Guided Spelling™

First edition published 2008.

Guided Spelling is a trademark of Center for the Collaborative Classroom.

Center for the Collaborative Classroom
1001 Marina Village Parkway, Suite 110
Alameda, CA 94501
(800) 666-7270; fax: (510) 464-3670
collaborativeclassroom.org

ISBN-13: 978-1-59892-778-8
ISBN-10: 1-59892-778-7

Printed in Canada

3 4 5 6 7 8 9 10 11 12 MQB 26 25 24 23 22 21 20 19 18

Contents

Guided Spelling Lessons

NEW WORDS

____	*1. add	When I add blue paint to yellow, I get green.
____	*2. led	The girl with the red hat led the way.
____	*3. with	He came to school with his sister.
____	*4. rich	The rich king had gold and silver.
____	5. fresh	Eat fresh fruits and vegetables.
____	6. which	She wondered which book to choose.
____	7. thick	They put on a thick coat of paint.
____	8. check	We will all check our work.
____	*9. cold	Mom told us it was cold outside.
____	*10. hold	Fold the paper and hold it up.
____	11. pull	We'll pull the wagon to the park.
____	12. full	The glass is half full.

Name: _____

1. _____

2. _____

3. _____

4. _____

1. _____

2. _____

3. _____

4. _____

5. _____

6. _____

hold

pull

full

cold

1. _____

2. _____

3. _____

4. _____

1. _____

2. _____

3. _____

4. _____

holds

pulls

full

5. _____   8. _____

6. _____   9. _____

7. _____   10. _____

Write words that have short **e**.

best

Write words that have short **i**.

drip

NEW WORDS

____ *1. box   The pencils are in a box.

____ *2. must   Dad said we must be careful.

____ *3. glad   They talked about being mad, sad, and glad.

____ *4. sand   I like to stand in the sand.

____ 5. song   We listened to a long song.

____ 6. still   They are still working in the garden.

____ 7. trip   His trip to the Grand Canyon was exciting.

____ 8. soft   The kitty loves her soft pillow.

____ *9. mother His mother and brother waited for him.

____ *10. other   Choose one or the other.

____ 11. month   The month of June has thirty days.

____ 12. laugh   Our funny baby makes us laugh.

REVIEW WORDS

____ *13. led   ____ 17. which   ____ *21. hold

____ *14. rich   ____ 18. fresh   ____ *22. cold

____ *15. add   ____ 19. check   ____ 23. full

____ *16. with   ____ 20. thick   ____ 24. pull

Challenge Words

____ 25. until   We talked until the bell rang.

____ 26. upon   Once upon a time there were seven sisters.

____ 27. begin   The picnic will begin at 11:00.

____ 28. began   Last year school began in September.

Name: _____

laugh

month

other

mother

1. _____

2. _____

3. _____

4. _____

5. _____

6. _____

7. _____

8. _____

1. _____

2. _____

3. _____

4. _____

5. _____

6. _____

7. _____

8. _____

9. _____

10. _____

there
pull
hold

Name: _____

1. _____

2. _____

3. _____

4. _____

5. _____

6. _____

7. _____

8. _____

9. _____

10. _____

mother

other

anyone

1. _____

2. _____

3. _____

4. _____

5. _____

6. _____

7. _____

month
Dr.
laugh

8. _____

9. _____

10. _____

Name:

Write words that have a short vowel and begin with one of these consonant clusters: **br-**, **cl-**, **cr-**, **dr-**, **fl-**, **fr-**, **gl-**, **gr-**, **pl-**, **pr-**, **sl-**, **sp-**, **st-**, **tr-**, **spl-**, or **str-**.

glass

splint

NEW WORDS

___	*1. plants	The plants in the pots are growing well.
___	*2. stands	The dancer stands up straight.
___	*3. kings	The kings rode out on their horses.
___	*4. milk	Please pour the milk.
___	5. flat	That flat mat is at the door.
___	6. kept	They kept the old books.
___	7. land	The pioneers crossed miles and miles of land.
___	8. held	I have held the puppy. Now you hold her.
___	*9. won't	If you don't hurry, you won't finish on time.
___	*10. mind	Use your mind to find the answer.
___	11. wind (2)	Wind up this plane and watch it fly in the wind.
___	12. group	Every group solved the problem.

REVIEW WORDS

___ *13. box	___ 17. soft	___ *21. other
___ *14. sand	___ 18. trip	___ *22. mother
___ *15. glad	___ 19. still	___ 23. laugh
___ *16. must	___ 20. song	___ 24. month

Challenge Words

___	25. person	Hand your paper to the person on your left.
___	26. hundred	One hundred centimeters equal one meter.
___	27. family	Their family went to the museum.
___	28. finger	She put the ring on her finger.

Name: _____

wind

mind

won't

group

1. _____

2. _____

3. _____

4. _____

5. _____

6. _____

7. _____

8. _____

1. _____

2. _____

3. _____

4. _____

5. _____

6. _____

7. _____

mother
laugh
others

8. _____

9. _____

10. _____

Name: _____

1. _____

2. _____

3. _____

4. _____

5. _____

6. _____

7. _____

8. _____

9. _____

10. _____

anybody
won't
mind

1. _____

2. _____

3. _____

4. _____

winds
Mr.
group

5. _____   8. _____

6. _____   9. _____

7. _____   10. _____

Write words that end with one of these consonant clusters: **-ft**, **-ld**, **-lk**, **-mp**, **-nch**, **-nd**, **-nk**, **-nt**, or **-st**.

bench

silk

NEW WORDS

____	*1. passes	The group leader passes out the paper.
____	*2. glasses	She sees better with glasses.
____	*3. facts	The class has read facts about the ocean.
____	*4. hands	The volunteers raised their hands.
____	5. length	The length of the field is 100 yards.
____	6. send	They like to send messages.
____	7. eggs	One of the eggs was cracked.
____	8. spent	They spent a month studying reptiles.
____	*9. also	Their grandparents came also.
____	*10. bought	We brought the food that we bought.
____	11. father	Their father showed them a new game.
____	12. toward	The bus came toward the bus stop.

REVIEW WORDS

____ *13. stands	____ 17. land	____ *21. mind
____ *14. milks	____ 18. flat	____ *22. won't
____ *15. kings	____ 19. held	____ 23. group
____ *16. plants	____ 20. kept	____ 24. wind (2)

Challenge Words

____	25. children	The children cut out decorations.
____	26. bottom	Tom swam to the bottom of the pool.
____	27. travel	Immigrants travel a long, long way.
____	28. ocean	Some parts of the ocean are shallow.

Name: _____

bought

also

toward

father

1. _____

2. _____

3. _____

4. _____

5. _____

6. _____

7. _____

8. _____

1. _____

2. _____

3. _____

4. _____

5. _____

6. _____

7. _____

won't

group

mind

8. _____

9. _____

10. _____

Name: _____

1. _____

2. _____

3. _____

4. _____

5. _____

6. _____

7. _____

also
bought
anywhere

8. _____

9. _____

10. _____

1. _____

2. _____

3. _____

4. _____

5. _____

6. _____

7. _____

toward
father
Miss

8. _____

9. _____

10. _____

Endings **s** and **es**

Name:

Write words that have the ending **s**.
Underline each base word.

<u>sits</u>

<u>wants</u>

Write words that have the ending **es**.
Underline each base word.

<u>classes</u>

<u>brushes</u>

Name: _____

NEW WORDS

___	*1. planned	The class planned a science experiment.
___	*2. missing	His pencil is missing again.
___	*3. dishes	They put the dishes on the shelf.
___	*4. sitting	The cat was sitting by the fire.
___	5. brings	The bird brings food to the nest.
___	6. grass	The grass turned brown in the fall.
___	7. sent	They sent a package to their grandparents.
___	8. lost	She lost her jacket at school.
___	*9. dead	Some of the flowers were dead.
___	*10. die	They watered the plant so it wouldn't die.
___	11. tie	Tie your shoelaces.
___	12. field	The soccer field was wet and muddy.

REVIEW WORDS

___ *13. hands	___ 17. length	___ *21. bought
___ *14. glasses	___ 18. eggs	___ *22. also
___ *15. passes	___ 19. spent	___ 23. toward
___ *16. facts	___ 20. send	___ 24. father

Challenge Words

___ 25. island	They took a boat to the island.
___ 26. picture	She drew a picture of the main character.
___ 27. forest	The wind blew through the forest trees.
___ 28. famous	Some people are famous for their inventions.

dead

field

tie

die

1. _____

2. _____

3. _____

4. _____

5. _____

6. _____

7. _____

8. _____

1. _____

2. _____

3. _____

4. _____

5. _____

6. _____

7. _____

8. _____

9. _____

10. _____

who's
toward
father

Name: _____

1. _____

2. _____

3. _____

4. _____

5. _____

6. _____

7. _____

8. _____

9. _____

10. _____

dead

ties

anything

Ms.
field
dies

1. _____

2. _____

3. _____

4. _____

5. _____ 8. _____

6. _____ 9. _____

7. _____ 10. _____

Name: _____

Write words that begin or end with **sh**, **ch**, **th**, or **wh**.

thank

Name:
_____

Week 1

____ *1. led
____ *2. rich
____ *3. add
____ *4. with
____ 5. which
____ 6. fresh
____ 7. check
____ 8. thick
____ *9. hold
____ *10. cold
____ 11. full
____ 12. pull

Week 2

____ *13. box
____ *14. sand
____ *15. glad
____ *16. must
____ 17. soft
____ 18. trip
____ 19. still
____ 20. song
____ *21. other
____ *22. mother
____ 23. laugh
____ 24. month

Week 3

____ *25. stands
____ *26. milk
____ *27. kings
____ *28. plants
____ 29. land
____ 30. flat
____ 31. held
____ 32. kept
____ *33. mind
____ *34. won't
____ 35. group
____ 36. wind (2)

Week 4

____ *37. hands
____ *38. glasses
____ *39. passes
____ *40. facts
____ 41. length
____ 42. eggs
____ 43. spent
____ 44. send
____ *45. bought
____ *46. also
____ 47. toward
____ 48. father

Challenge Words

Week 2
upon, began, until, begin

Week 3
finger, family, hundred, person

Week 4
bottom, children, travel, ocean

Name: _____

1. _____

2. _____

3. _____

4. _____

5. _____

6. _____

7. _____

8. _____

9. _____

10. _____

11. _____

12. _____

1. They bougt fresh milk and eggs.

2. The box held a thick, soft pillow for the cat.

3. Wich math facs have you learned this munth?

4. My fother and muther wo'nt mind if I hold the snake.

5. She lost her glases, and they are stil missing.

Name: _____

Write these words in alphabetical order:

length, facts, pull, bought, month, won't, hands, eggs, glasses, kept

1. _____

2. _____

3. _____

4. _____

5. _____

6. _____

7. _____

8. _____

9. _____

10. _____

Name: _____

NEW WORDS

___	*1. match	We need a match to light the fire.
___	*2. edge	The swimmers dove from the edge of the pool.
___	*3. wrong	She called the wrong number.
___	*4. cross	Cross every **t**.
___	5. bridge	We cross the bridge to go to the city.
___	6. sticks	This tape sticks well.
___	7. felt	It felt hot in the sun.
___	8. scratch	The new desk did not have a scratch on it.
___	*9. head	We have read about the owl's head.
___	*10. would	I would go if I could.
___	11. should	You should be careful on the monkey bars.
___	12. school	Fifth and sixth graders go to that school.

REVIEW WORDS

___ *13. dishes	___ 17. grass	___ *21. die
___ *14. planned	___ 18. brings	___ *22. dead
___ *15. sitting	___ 19. lost	___ 23. field
___ *16. missing	___ 20. sent	___ 24. tie

Challenge Words

___	25. broken	The old bicycle was broken.
___	26. kitchen	He went to the kitchen for a snack.
___	27. motion	They watched the motion of the fish's fins.
___	28. corner	The pointer is kept in the corner.

head

should

would

school

1. _____

2. _____

3. _____

4. _____

5. _____

6. _____

7. _____

8. _____

1. _____

2. _____

3. _____

4. _____

5. _____

6. _____

7. _____

8. _____

9. _____

10. _____

field
you'll
dies

Name: _____

1. _____

2. _____

3. _____

4. _____

5. _____

6. _____

7. _____

8. _____

9. _____

10. _____

head

would

someone

1. _____

2. _____

3. _____

4. _____

5. _____

6. _____

7. _____

Mrs.
should
would

8. _____

9. _____

10. _____

Words That End with **ng**

Write words that end with **ang**.

<u>sprang</u> _____

_____

_____

_____

Write words that end with **ing**.

<u>wing</u> _____

_____

_____

_____

Write words that end with **ong**.

_____

_____

_____

_____

Write words that end with **ung**.

_____

_____

_____

_____

NEW WORDS

___	*1. fifty	Two times fifty equals one hundred.
___	*2. plenty	There is plenty of food for everyone.
___	*3. happy	She was happy when school started.
___	*4. quickly	The class lined up quickly.
___	5. body	The body of a whale is huge.
___	6. empty	The bottle was empty.
___	7. funny	Their uncle tells funny jokes.
___	8. judge	The judge listened carefully to everyone.
___	*9. gold	He told me I could hold a piece of gold.
___	*10. push	Push the desks to the side.
___	11. floor	They cleaned the door and the floor.
___	12. break	The plastic cup won't break.

REVIEW WORDS

___ *13. wrong	___ 17. sticks	___ *21. would
___ *14. cross	___ 18. bridge	___ *22. head
___ *15. edge	___ 19. scratch	___ 23. school
___ *16. match	___ 20. felt	___ 24. should

Challenge Words

___	25. hungry	The food was nibbled by hungry mice.
___	26. angry	The angry child stamped his foot.
___	27. sorry	I'm sorry that I dropped the glass.
___	28. industry	The footwear industry produces shoes and boots.

Name: _____

push

gold

break

floor

1. _____

2. _____

3. _____

4. _____

5. _____

6. _____

7. _____

8. _____

1. _____

2. _____

3. _____

4. _____

5. _____

6. _____

7. _____

8. _____

9. _____

10. _____

head
you're
would

Name: _____

1. _____

2. _____

3. _____

4. _____

5. _____

6. _____

7. _____

8. _____

9. _____

10. _____

break

goldfish

pushes

1. _____

2. _____

3. _____

4. _____

floors

Ave.

gold

5. _____   8. _____

6. _____   9. _____

7. _____   10. _____

How Many Syllables?

Write words that have more than one syllable. After each word, write the number of syllables in the word.

kangaroo 3

chapter 2

NEW WORDS

___ *1. gave   I gave my dog a biscuit.

___ *2. nine   Her sister turned nine today.

___ *3. page   The page had a beautiful illustration.

___ *4. phone   The ringing phone woke us up.

___ 5. live (2)   Live snails can live in the tank.

___ 6. inside   We stayed inside because of the rain.

___ 7. change   They always change their clothes after school.

___ 8. strange   The sudden change in weather was strange.

___ *9. pretty   The flowers by the road are pretty.

___ *10. chief   The chief is the leader.

___ 11. clothes   Clothes are usually made of cloth.

___ 12. shoes   I tied my little brother's shoes.

REVIEW WORDS

___ *13. plenty   ___ 17. empty   ___ *21. push

___ *14. quickly   ___ 18. body   ___ *22. gold

___ *15. happy   ___ 19. judge   ___ 23. break

___ *16. fifty   ___ 20. funny   ___ 24. floor

Challenge Words

___ 25. perhaps   Perhaps we'll go to the zoo.

___ 26. special   The bus was towed by a special truck.

___ 27. complete   He didn't complete his work on time.

___ 28. paragraph   The last paragraph was a surprise.

Name: _____

clothes

pretty

shoes

chief

1. _____

2. _____

3. _____

4. _____

5. _____

6. _____

7. _____

8. _____

1. _____

2. _____

3. _____

4. _____

push

gold

weren't

5. _____   8. _____

6. _____   9. _____

7. _____   10. _____

1. _____

2. _____

3. _____

4. _____

5. _____

6. _____

7. _____

8. _____

9. _____

10. _____

wristwatch

shoes

chief

1. _____

2. _____

3. _____

4. _____

5. _____

6. _____

7. _____

8. _____

9. _____

10. _____

pretty
clothes
St.

Write words that have a short vowel.

odd

split

Write words that have a long vowel *and* have **e** at the end.

rope

prize

NEW WORDS

____	*1. cent	He didn't have a cent left.
____	*2. city	The city of New York has many tall buildings.
____	*3. fancy	They made fancy decorations for the party.
____	*4. sixty	Sixty divided by two equals thirty.
____	5. rocks	There were many rocks in the geology display.
____	6. strong	A strong wind blew the tree over.
____	7. thin	We can use thin paper for tracing.
____	8. pencil	This pencil has a new eraser.
____	*9. chance	There is a chance of rain.
____	*10. sign	The sign told the name of the street.
____	11. since	It was a long time since the prince had left.
____	12. few	She threw a few vegetables into the stew.

REVIEW WORDS

____ *13. gave	____ 17. inside	____ *21. chief
____ *14. phone	____ 18. live (2)	____ *22. pretty
____ *15. page	____ 19. strange	____ 23. shoes
____ *16. nine	____ 20. change	____ 24. clothes

Challenge Words

____	25. center	The game starts in the center.
____	26. science	Many scientists study science all their lives.
____	27. except	She spelled all the words except one.
____	28. century	A century is 100 years.

chance

sign

few

since

1. _____

2. _____

3. _____

4. _____

5. _____

6. _____

7. _____

8. _____

1. _____

2. _____

3. _____

4. _____

what's
clothes
chief

5. _____ 8. _____

6. _____ 9. _____

7. _____ 10. _____

Name: _____

1. _____

2. _____

3. _____

4. _____

5. _____

6. _____

7. _____

since

somebody

chance

8. _____

9. _____

10. _____

1. _____

2. _____

3. _____

4. _____

5. _____

6. _____

7. _____

Rd.

few

sign

8. _____

9. _____

10. _____

Name: _____

Write words that have the letter **c**. Underline every **c** that has the sound of **s**.

spa<u>c</u>e _____   _____

color _____   _____

_____   _____

_____   _____

_____   _____

_____   _____

_____   _____

_____   _____

NEW WORDS

___	*1. feet	Hippopotamuses' feet are good for walking in mud.
___	*2. mean	You mean you want us to clean?
___	*3. read (2)	Now we'll read again what we read yesterday.
___	*4. need	We need to feed seeds to our bird.
___	5. near	He is near enough to hear you.
___	6. fifteen	Fifteen and thirty-five are fifty.
___	7. three	Three bees buzzed around my knees.
___	8. sea	The seals swam in the sea.
___	*9. country	They came from a country far away.
___	*10. half	The calf ate half the hay.
___	11. health	After her broken leg healed, she was in good health.
___	12. breath	She took a big breath of fresh air.

REVIEW WORDS

___ *13. sixty	___ 17. pencil	___ *21. sign
___ *14. cent	___ 18. strong	___ *22. chance
___ *15. fancy	___ 19. thin	___ 23. few
___ *16. city	___ 20. rocks	___ 24. since

Challenge Words

___	25. between	A bookmark is between the pages.
___	26. reason	Bad weather was the reason we stayed in.
___	27. easy	That puzzle isn't easy!
___	28. easily	We just can't do it easily.

Name: _____

half

country

breath

health

1. _____   5. _____

2. _____   6. _____

3. _____   7. _____

4. _____   8. _____

1. _____

2. _____

3. _____

4. _____

5. _____

6. _____

7. _____

chance
I'm
since

8. _____

9. _____

10. _____

Name: _____

1. _____

2. _____

3. _____

4. _____

5. _____ 8. _____

6. _____ 9. _____

7. _____ 10. _____

health
half
chance

1. _____

2. _____

3. _____

4. _____

5. _____

6. _____

7. _____

country

lb.

breath

8. _____

9. _____

10. _____

Name: _____

Which words this week did you need to study?

_____   _____

_____   _____

_____   _____

_____   _____

_____   _____

_____   _____

_____   _____

_____   _____

Name:

Week 5

____ *1. dishes
____ *2. planned
____ *3. sitting
____ *4. missing
____ 5. grass
____ 6. brings
____ 7. lost
____ 8. sent
____ *9. die
____ *10. dead
____ 11. field
____ 12. tie

Week 7

____ *13. wrong
____ *14. cross
____ *15. edge
____ *16. match
____ 17. sticks
____ 18. bridge
____ 19. scratch
____ 20. felt
____ *21. would
____ *22. head
____ 23. school
____ 24. should

Week 8

____ *25. plenty
____ *26. quickly
____ *27. happy
____ *28. fifty
____ 29. empty
____ 30. body
____ 31. judge
____ 32. funny
____ *33. push
____ *34. gold
____ 35. break
____ 36. floor

Week 9

____ *37. gave
____ *38. phone
____ *39. page
____ *40. nine
____ 41. inside
____ 42. live (2)
____ 43. strange
____ 44. change
____ *45. chief
____ *46. pretty
____ 47. shoes
____ 48. clothes

Week 10

____ *49. sixty
____ *50. cent
____ *51. fancy
____ *52. city
____ 53. pencil
____ 54. strong
____ 55. thin
____ 56. rocks
____ *57. sign
____ *58. chance
____ 59. few
____ 60. since

Challenge Words

Week 5
forest, island, famous, picture

Week 7
motion, kitchen, corner, broken

Week 8
industry, hungry, sorry, angry

Week 9
special, complete, perhaps, paragraph

Week 10
except, center, science, century

Name: _____

1. _____

2. _____

3. _____

4. _____

5. _____

6. _____

7. _____

8. _____

9. _____

10. _____

11. _____

12. _____

1. The dishs may fall off the edge and brake on the flore.

2. They went to the city to buy new close and shoos for school.

3. We thought we had pletty of pincels but the box was emty.

4. Change your answer if it is wrong.

5. Strage lizards liv among the rocks.

Alphabetical Order

Write these words in alphabetical order. In some words, you will need to look at the first and second letters:

strange, **pencil**, **clothes**, **body**, **would**, **city**, **head**, **phone**, **wrong**, **bridge**

1. _____

2. _____

3. _____

4. _____

5. _____

6. _____

7. _____

8. _____

9. _____

10. _____

NEW WORDS

___	*1. shapes	We cut out five-sided shapes.
___	*2. chased	The kitten chased the ball across the room.
___	*3. writing	She is writing a report about windmills.
___	*4. September	The first day of fall is in September.
___	5. cares	He cares for his brother, so he shares with him.
___	6. used (2)	He used the hammer that used to be his dad's.
___	7. racing	The runners were racing toward the finish line.
___	8. shared	She shared the cherries with everyone.
___	*9. lose	I didn't want to lose my locket, but it's lost.
___	*10. loose	The goose got loose.
___	11. living	The family was living in Rhode Island.
___	12. across	The store is across the street.

REVIEW WORDS

___ *13. feet	___ 17. fifteen	___ *21. half
___ *14. read (2)	___ 18. sea	___ *22. country
___ *15. need	___ 19. near	___ 23. breath
___ *16. mean	___ 20. three	___ 24. health

Challenge Words

___ 25. common	Robins are common in many places.
___ 26. problem	One multiplication problem was very difficult.
___ 27. written	We have written in our journals each week.
___ 28. suddenly	Suddenly we heard a loud noise.

living

lose

loose

across

1. _____

2. _____

3. _____

4. _____

5. _____

6. _____

7. _____

8. _____

1. _____

2. _____

3. _____

4. _____

5. _____

6. _____

7. _____

8. _____

9. _____

10. _____

half
he'll
country

Name: _____

1. _____

2. _____

3. _____

4. _____

5. _____

6. _____

7. _____

8. _____

9. _____

10. _____

lose

somewhere

loose

1. _____

2. _____

3. _____

4. _____

5. _____

6. _____

7. _____

living
across
Sept.

8. _____

9. _____

10. _____

Write words that rhyme with **squeak**. They may end with **eak** or **eek**. Underline each word that ends with **eak**.

<u>creak</u>

<u>sleek</u>

NEW WORDS

____ *1. under   The bug lived under the rock.

____ *2. bird   The bird flew hundreds of miles.

____ *3. burn   They watched the candle burn.

____ *4. third   The third chapter is about wheels.

____ 5. first   We hung up our jackets first.

____ 6. during   He hurt his foot during recess.

____ 7. feel   Does your sister feel better today?

____ 8. eat   Their mother told them to be neat when they eat.

____ *9. wear   She wants to wear this shirt, but it has a tear.

____ *10. worse   The weather was bad yesterday but is worse today.

____ 11. worst   It was the worst weather they had ever seen.

____ 12. search   Let's search for the lost toy.

REVIEW WORDS

____ *13. chased   ____ 17. cares   ____ *21. loose

____ *14. September   ____ 18. racing   ____ *22. lose

____ *15. shapes   ____ 19. used (2)   ____ 23. across

____ *16. writing   ____ 20. shared   ____ 24. living

Challenge Words

____ 25. surface   The surface of the water was smooth.

____ 26. return   Return the permission slip to the teacher.

____ 27. modern   A modern building was beside the old building.

____ 28. interest   The class read about bats with interest.

Name: _____

search

worse

worst

wear

1. _____

2. _____

3. _____

4. _____

5. _____

6. _____

7. _____

8. _____

1. _____

2. _____

3. _____

4. _____

5. _____

6. _____

7. _____

we're

across

loose

8. _____

9. _____

10. _____

1. _____

2. _____

3. _____

4. _____

5. _____

6. _____

7. _____

searches
living
wears

8. _____

9. _____

10. _____

1. _____

2. _____

3. _____

4. _____

5. _____

6. _____

7. _____

USA

worst

worse

8. _____

9. _____

10. _____

Words I Already Knew

Which words this week did you already know how to spell?

_____   _____

_____   _____

_____   _____

_____   _____

_____   _____

_____   _____

_____   _____

NEW WORDS

____	*1. March	The first day of spring is in March.
____	*2. horse	She wished she had her own horse.
____	*3. store	The hardware store sells many kinds of tools.
____	*4. large	Large clouds filled the sky.
____	5. October	The weather was cool in October.
____	6. forty	Bring forty forks for the picnic.
____	7. before	Wash your hands before you eat.
____	8. north	The compass needle always points north.
____	*9. fourteen	*Fourteen* begins like *four* and *fourth*.
____	*10. climb	She likes to climb the bars to the top.
____	11. prove	They wanted to prove that they were right.
____	12. fourth	He was fourth in line.

REVIEW WORDS

____ *13. third	____ 17. during	____ *21. worse
____ *14. burn	____ 18. eat	____ *22. wear
____ *15. bird	____ 19. first	____ 23. search
____ *16. under	____ 20. feel	____ 24. worst

Challenge Words

____ 25. dollar	A dollar can be a bill or a coin.
____ 26. similar	A donkey is similar to a horse.
____ 27. doctor	A veterinarian is an animal doctor.
____ 28. information	We looked for information in the encyclopedia.

Name: _____

prove

fourteen

climb

fourth

1. _____   5. _____

2. _____   6. _____

3. _____   7. _____

4. _____   8. _____

1. _____

2. _____

3. _____

4. _____

5. _____

6. _____

7. _____

8. _____

9. _____

10. _____

search

worse

she'll

Name: _____

1. _____

2. _____

3. _____

4. _____

5. _____

6. _____

7. _____

fourteen

something

climbed

8. _____

9. _____

10. _____

1. _____

2. _____

3. _____

4. _____

Mar.

proves

fourth

5. _____   8. _____

6. _____   9. _____

7. _____   10. _____

Name: _____

Which words in this week do you use the most in your writing?

_____   _____

_____   _____

_____   _____

_____   _____

_____   _____

NEW WORDS

___	*1. wait	Please wait in a straight line.
___	*2. May	April showers bring May flowers.
___	*3. Thursday	He has a dentist appointment on Thursday.
___	*4. Saturday	We went to the game on Saturday.
___	5. main	The brain is the main part of the head.
___	6. hair	Feel the air blow through your hair.
___	7. over	She taught her dog to roll over.
___	8. those	I chose those roses.
___	*9. Monday	We're presenting our play on Monday.
___	*10. none	Three, two, one, none!
___	11. eighteen	Its weight is eighteen pounds.
___	12. straight	Use the ruler to draw a straight line.

REVIEW WORDS

___ *13. horse	___ 17. north	___ *21. climb
___ *14. large	___ 18. forty	___ *22. fourteen
___ *15. store	___ 19. before	___ 23. fourth
___ *16. March	___ 20. October	___ 24. prove

Challenge Words

___ 25. explain	Please explain this sentence to us.
___ 26. afraid	She's not afraid to dive into the pool.
___ 27. always	It's always daylight somewhere on earth.
___ 28. maybe	Maybe the new supplies will arrive tomorrow.

Name: _____

Monday

straight

eighteen

1. _____

2. _____

3. _____

4. _____

5. _____

6. _____

7. _____

8. _____

1. _____

2. _____

3. _____

4. _____

5. _____

6. _____

7. _____

fourth
let's
proved

8. _____

9. _____

10. _____

Name: _____

1. _____

2. _____

3. _____

4. _____

climb
straight
eighteen

5. _____   8. _____

6. _____   9. _____

7. _____   10. _____

1. _____

2. _____

3. _____

4. _____

5. _____

6. _____

7. _____

Oct.
Monday
none

8. _____

9. _____

10. _____

Rhymes for **fin** and **fine**

Write words that rhyme with **fin**.

grin

Write words that rhyme with **fine**.

whine

NEW WORDS

____	*1. boat	I hope my paper boat will float.
____	*2. low	We searched high and low for the missing book.
____	*3. grow	Some trees grow very slowly.
____	*4. November	The month of November has 30 days.
____	5. throat	The doctor looked at my sore throat.
____	6. snow	The wind may blow the snow away.
____	7. board	He sawed the board into four pieces.
____	8. note	My mother wrote a note to the teacher.
____	*9. due	The library book is due on Tuesday.
____	*10. truth	She always tells the truth.
____	11. toe	My dog stepped on my toe.
____	12. along	Sing the song along with me.

REVIEW WORDS

____ *13. Thursday	____ 17. those	____ *21. none
____ *14. wait	____ 18. main	____ *22. Monday
____ *15. Saturday	____ 19. over	____ 23. straight
____ *16. May	____ 20. hair	____ 24. eighteen

Challenge Words

____ 25. below	Below ground the seeds began to grow.
____ 26. follow	Follow me!
____ 27. window	The sun shines through the window.
____ 28. machine	One machine may do several jobs.

Name: _____

due

toe

truth

along

1. _____

2. _____

3. _____

4. _____

5. _____

6. _____

7. _____

8. _____

Name:

1. _____

2. _____

3. _____

4. _____

5. _____

6. _____

7. _____

8. _____

9. _____

10. _____

can't
straight
Monday

Name: _____

1. _____

2. _____

3. _____

4. _____

5. _____

6. _____

7. _____

8. _____

9. _____

10. _____

eighteen
along
toenail

1. _____

2. _____

3. _____

4. _____

5. _____   8. _____

6. _____   9. _____

7. _____   10. _____

due
Nov.
truth

Name:

Write words that rhyme with **stair**. They may end with **air** or **are**. Underline each word that ends with **air**.

flare

<u>fair</u>

Name:

_____

Week 11

___ *1. feet
___ *2. read (2)
___ *3. need
___ *4. mean
___ 5. fifteen
___ 6. sea
___ 7. near
___ 8. three
___ *9. half
___ *10. country
___ 11. breath
___ 12. health

Week 13

___ *13. chased
___ *14. September
___ *15. shapes
___ *16. writing
___ 17. cares
___ 18. racing
___ 19. used (2)
___ 20. shared
___ *21. loose
___ *22. lose
___ 23. across
___ 24. living

Week 14

___ *25. third
___ *26. burn
___ *27. bird
___ *28. under
___ 29. during
___ 30. eat
___ 31. first
___ 32. feel
___ *33. worse
___ *34. wear
___ 35. search
___ 36. worst

Week 15

___ *37. horse
___ *38. large
___ *39. store
___ *40. March
___ 41. north
___ 42. forty
___ 43. before
___ 44. October
___ *45. climb
___ *46. fourteen
___ 47. fourth
___ 48. prove

Week 16

___ *49. Thursday
___ *50. wait
___ *51. Saturday
___ *52. May
___ 53. those
___ 54. main
___ 55. over
___ 56. hair
___ *57. none
___ *58. Monday
___ 59. straight
___ 60. eighteen

Challenge Words

Week 11
easily, between, easy, reason

Week 13
problem, common, suddenly, written

Week 14
surface, modern, interest, return

Week 15
dollar, doctor, information, similar

Week 16
maybe, always, afraid, explain

Name: _____

1. _____

2. _____

3. _____

4. _____

5. _____

6. _____

7. _____

8. _____

9. _____

10. _____

11. _____

12. _____

_____

1. Last thirsday we saw a large bird neer the store.

_____

2. We used a ruler to draw forteen straiht lines.

_____

3. Their goose got loose, so they had to serch far and nere.

_____

4. They were driving accross the cuntry from Munday until Saturday.

_____

5. We nead to read our writing carefully.

Name: _____

Write these words in alphabetical order. In some words, you will need to look at the first, second, and third letters:

need, fourth, straight, lose, search, loose, country, near, forty, eighteen

1. _____

2. _____

3. _____

4. _____

5. _____

6. _____

7. _____

8. _____

9. _____

10. _____

NEW WORDS

____ *1. starring   Our favorite actor is starring in the movie.

____ *2. stayed   The cat stayed indoors.

____ *3. closing   We're closing the door now.

____ *4. Friday   Friday was the last day of our science unit.

____ 5. marked   The teacher's assistant marked the papers.

____ 6. states   They saw license plates from 50 states.

____ 7. raised   The flags were raised each morning.

____ 8. tail   The monkey was hanging by its tail.

____ *9. instead   We read one long book instead of two short ones.

____ *10. sold   The store sold clothes and shoes.

____ 11. fold   Fold your paper from bottom to top.

____ 12. worth   He thought the old jar was worth nothing.

REVIEW WORDS

____ *13. boat   ____ 17. note   ____ *21. truth

____ *14. November   ____ 18. throat   ____ *22. due

____ *15. grow   ____ 19. board   ____ 23. along

____ *16. low   ____ 20. snow   ____ 24. toe

Challenge Words

____ 25. either   You may choose either or neither of them.

____ 26. moment   We saw the shooting star for a moment.

____ 27. product   That factory produces several products.

____ 28. present (2) They wanted to present a beautiful present to their teacher.

fold

instead

sold

worth

1. _____

2. _____

3. _____

4. _____

5. _____

6. _____

7. _____

8. _____

1. _____

2. _____

3. _____

4. _____

5. _____

6. _____

7. _____

8. _____

9. _____

10. _____

it'll
along
truth

Name: _____

1. _____

2. _____

3. _____

4. _____

5. _____

6. _____

7. _____

8. _____

9. _____

10. _____

instead

toe

worth

1. _____

2. _____

3. _____

4. _____

5. _____

6. _____

7. _____

8. _____

9. _____

10. _____

sold

folding

Fri.

Name: _____

Which words this week were easy for you to learn?

_____   _____

_____   _____

_____   _____

_____   _____

_____   _____

_____   _____

_____   _____

_____   _____

NEW WORDS

____ *1. soon   Spring would soon arrive.

____ *2. grew   The bird grew strong and flew away.

____ *3. June   The longest day of the year is in June.

____ *4. Sunday   Sunday afternoon they went for a run.

____ 5. moon   The moon was in the sky at noon.

____ 6. choose   Which color of paint shall we choose?

____ 7. team   The team practiced long and hard.

____ 8. knew   She knew all the presidents in order.

____ *9. Tuesday   On Tuesday they began studying machines.

____ *10. fruit   Oranges and lemons are citrus fruit.

____ 11. suit   He likes his new suit.

____ 12. whose   Whose team will win, and whose team will lose?

REVIEW WORDS

____ *13. closing   ____ 17. marked   ____ *21. sold

____ *14. starring   ____ 18. tail   ____ *22. instead

____ *15. Friday   ____ 19. states   ____ 23. worth

____ *16. stayed   ____ 20. raised   ____ 24. fold

Challenge Words

____ 25. history   History is the story of people.

____ 26. human   Every woman and man is human.

____ 27. object   Our assignment was to describe an object.

____ 28. subject   My favorite subject is math.

Name: _____

Tuesday

fruit

whose

suit

1. _____

2. _____

3. _____

4. _____

5. _____

6. _____

7. _____

8. _____

1. _____

2. _____

3. _____

4. _____

5. _____

6. _____

7. _____

8. _____

9. _____

10. _____

doesn't
folded
instead

1. _____

2. _____

3. _____

4. _____

5. _____   8. _____

6. _____   9. _____

7. _____   10. _____

whose

worth

suits

1. _____

2. _____

3. _____

4. _____

5. _____

6. _____

7. _____

8. _____

9. _____

10. _____

Tuesday
fruit
Mon.

Name: _____

Which words this week did you need to study?

_____   _____

_____   _____

_____   _____

_____   _____

_____   _____

_____   _____

_____   _____

_____   _____

NEW WORDS

____	*1. book	Did you look through the book?
____	*2. stood	They stood quietly and waited.
____	*3. foot	He hurt his foot in the game.
____	*4. woods	There was an old cabin in the woods.
____	5. fire	The fire in the fireplace kept them warm.
____	6. thirteen	*Thirteen* begins like *third* and *thirty*.
____	7. heated	Our mother heated our supper in the oven.
____	8. street	The street had tall trees on both sides.
____	*9. guess	Just make a good guess.
____	*10. guard	My puppy likes to guard the yard.
____	11. guide	The teacher will guide us in spelling.
____	12. early	The sky is gray in the early morning.

REVIEW WORDS

____ *13. Sunday	____ 17. choose	____ *21. fruit
____ *14. June	____ 18. team	____ *22. Tuesday
____ *15. grew	____ 19. moon	____ 23. whose
____ *16. soon	____ 20. knew	____ 24. suit

Challenge Words

____ 25. describe	Describe the habitat of penguins.
____ 26. difficult	The last math problem is always difficult.
____ 27. develop	We wondered how the plot would develop.
____ 28. result	The result of the experiment was a surprise.

guide

guard

early

guess

1. _____

2. _____

3. _____

4. _____

5. _____

6. _____

7. _____

8. _____

Name:

_____

1. _____

2. _____

3. _____

4. _____

she's
Tuesday
fruit

5. _____   8. _____

6. _____   9. _____

7. _____   10. _____

Name: _____

1. _____

2. _____

3. _____

4. _____

5. _____

6. _____

7. _____

8. _____

9. _____

10. _____

guesses
whose
early

1. _____

2. _____

3. _____

4. _____

5. _____

6. _____

7. _____

Sun.

guided

guards

8. _____

9. _____

10. _____

Words I Already Knew

Which words this week did you already know how to spell?

_____   _____

_____   _____

_____   _____

_____   _____

_____   _____

_____   _____

_____   _____

_____   _____

NEW WORDS

____ *1. light   We needed a bright light.

____ *2. fry   He likes to fry vegetables.

____ *3. night   The stars shone beautifully that night.

____ *4. white   Write on white paper today.

____ 5. quite   The baby took quite a long nap.

____ 6. fine   Everyone did a fine job on the recycling project.

____ 7. sight   Many people without sight use guide dogs.

____ 8. sky   The sky grew dark and stormy.

____ *9. key   The right key will unlock the door.

____ *10. money   His grandfather gave him money to spend at the fair.

____ 11. English   English spelling can be a challenge.

____ 12. carry   Their job is to carry the play equipment.

REVIEW WORDS

____ *13. foot   ____ 17. thirteen   ____ *21. guard

____ *14. book   ____ 18. heated   ____ *22. guess

____ *15. woods   ____ 19. fire   ____ 23. early

____ *16. stood   ____ 20. street   ____ 24. guide

Challenge Words

____ 25. already   I had already left when I remembered my backpack.

____ 26. beside   The dictionary is beside the encyclopedia.

____ 27. practice   Let's practice our lines for the play.

____ 28. minute   Please wait a minute.

Name: _____

carry

key

English

money

1. _____

2. _____

3. _____

4. _____

5. _____

6. _____

7. _____

8. _____

1. _____

2. _____

3. _____

4. _____

5. _____

6. _____

7. _____

early

guard

they're

8. _____

9. _____

10. _____

Name: _____

1. _____

2. _____

3. _____

4. _____

5. _____

6. _____

7. _____

8. _____

9. _____

10. _____

carry

guessed

money

1. _____

2. _____

3. _____

4. _____

5. _____

6. _____

7. _____

8. _____

9. _____

10. _____

keys
Tues.
English

Which words this week were easy for you to learn?

_____   _____

_____   _____

_____   _____

_____   _____

_____   _____

_____   _____

_____   _____

NEW WORDS

____ *1. fries   She fries tomatoes and eggs for breakfast.

____ *2. cried   The baby cried when he was hungry.

____ *3. flying   Many geese were flying south.

____ *4. puppies   The puppies were asleep beside their mother.

____ 5. hurrying   They were hurrying to school.

____ 6. speed   A cheetah runs at a fast speed.

____ 7. week   They fed the neighbor's cat all week.

____ 8. speak   The teacher asked us to speak softly.

____ *9. ready   We were ready on time today.

____ *10. often   Planets can often be seen at night.

____ 11. listen   Service dogs listen carefully to instructions.

____ 12. become   A tadpole will become a frog.

REVIEW WORDS

____ *13. night   ____ 17. fine   ____ *21. money

____ *14. fry   ____ 18. quite   ____ *22. key

____ *15. white   ____ 19. sky   ____ 23. carry

____ *16. light   ____ 20. sight   ____ 24. English

Challenge Words

____ 25. level   The old floor was no longer level.

____ 26. rather   I would rather sing than dance.

____ 27. system   Our heart is part of our circulatory system.

____ 28. position   I am in a sitting position.

Name: _____

listen

ready

often

become

1. _____

2. _____

3. _____

4. _____

5. _____

6. _____

7. _____

8. _____

1. _____

2. _____

3. _____

4. _____

5. _____

6. _____

7. _____

8. _____

9. _____

10. _____

it's
English
money

Name: _____

1. _____

2. _____

3. _____

4. _____

5. _____

6. _____

7. _____

8. _____

9. _____

10. _____

listens

ready

nobody

1. _____

2. _____

3. _____

4. _____

5. _____

6. _____

7. _____

often
Thurs.
becomes

8. _____

9. _____

10. _____

Name: _____

Which words this week did you need to study?

_____   _____

_____   _____

_____   _____

_____   _____

_____   _____

_____   _____

_____   _____

_____   _____

Name: _____

Week 17

____ *1. boat
____ *2. November
____ *3. grow
____ *4. low
____ 5. note
____ 6. throat
____ 7. board
____ 8. snow
____ *9. truth
____ *10. due
____ 11. along
____ 12. toe

Week 19

____ *13. closing
____ *14. starring
____ *15. Friday
____ *16. stayed
____ 17. marked
____ 18. tail
____ 19. states
____ 20. raised
____ *21. sold
____ *22. instead
____ 23. worth
____ 24. fold

Week 20

____ *25. Sunday
____ *26. June
____ *27. grew
____ *28. soon
____ 29. choose
____ 30. team
____ 31. moon
____ 32. knew
____ *33. fruit
____ *34. Tuesday
____ 35. whose
____ 36. suit

Week 21

____ *37. foot
____ *38. book
____ *39. woods
____ *40. stood
____ 41. thirteen
____ 42. heated
____ 43. fire
____ 44. street
____ *45. guard
____ *46. guess
____ 47. early
____ 48. guide

Week 22

____ *49. night
____ *50. fry
____ *51. white
____ *52. light
____ 53. fine
____ 54. quite
____ 55. sky
____ 56. sight
____ *57. money
____ *58. key
____ 59. carry
____ 60. English

Challenge Words

Week 17
follow, window, machine, below

Week 19
product, moment, present (2), either

Week 20
history, subject, human, object

Week 21
difficult, develop, describe, result

Week 22
already, minute, practice, beside

Name: _____

1. _____

2. _____

3. _____

4. _____

5. _____

6. _____

7. _____

8. _____

9. _____

10. _____

11. _____

12. _____

Name:

_____

1. That night the fier heeted the cabin and gave us lite.

_____

2. Guess whose teem won on Friday.

_____

3. Use this mony to buy the frute before it is all sold.

_____

4. Your book is do on Friday, November 2.

_____

5. The mune was shining on the wight snow along our streat.

Write these words in alphabetical order. In some words, you will need to look at the first, second, third, and fourth letters:

guide, whose, English, board, raised, boat, starring, guard, early, stayed

1. _____

2. _____

3. _____

4. _____

5. _____

6. _____

7. _____

8. _____

9. _____

10. _____

NEW WORDS

____ *1. now   Now we know the answer.

____ *2. town   They moved to another town.

____ *3. house   The story was about a mouse in a house.

____ *4. hour   The program lasted one hour.

____ 5. brown   The new boots were brown.

____ 6. about   What were they shouting about?

____ 7. south   He searched north, south, east, and west.

____ 8. sound   The sound of the traffic was very loud.

____ *9. bread   She spread jam on her bread.

____ *10. meant   They figured out what the message meant.

____ 11. sense   Taste is one sense.

____ 12. weather   We expected hot weather in summer.

REVIEW WORDS

____ *13. flying   ____ 17. week   ____ *21. often

____ *14. fries   ____ 18. hurrying   ____ *22. ready

____ *15. puppies   ____ 19. speak   ____ 23. become

____ *16. cried   ____ 20. speed   ____ 24. listen

Challenge Words

____ 25. mountains   The mountains were covered with snow.

____ 26. thousand   Two thousand pounds equals a ton.

____ 27. flower   Bees carry pollen from flower to flower.

____ 28. flour   The bread was made from wheat and oat flour.

Name: _____

sense

bread

weather

meant

1. _____

2. _____

3. _____

4. _____

5. _____

6. _____

7. _____

8. _____

1. _____

2. _____

3. _____

4. _____

ready
we'll
often

5. _____   8. _____

6. _____   9. _____

7. _____   10. _____

Name: _____

1. _____

2. _____

3. _____

4. _____

5. _____

6. _____

7. _____

8. _____

9. _____

10. _____

listening

senses

meant

1. _____

2. _____

3. _____

4. _____

5. _____

6. _____

7. _____

Sat.
bread
weather

8. _____

9. _____

10. _____

Write words that rhyme with **pound**.	Write words that rhyme with **down**.	Write words that rhyme with **cow**.
mound	gown	plow
_____	_____	_____
_____	_____	_____
_____	_____	_____
_____	_____	_____

NEW WORDS

____ *1. boy's   The boy's pencil is sharp.

____ *2. boys'   The boys' dog followed them.

____ *3. men's   The men's team played every week.

____ *4. puppy's   The puppy's paws are white.

____ 5. puppies'   The puppies' mother protected them.

____ 6. girl's   Everyone in the girl's family came to the show.

____ 7. please   Please don't tease your sister.

____ 8. seem   The plants seem dry today. Let's water them.

____ *9. nothing   There was nothing in the bag.

____ *10. rough   They wore tough boots to hike on the rough trail.

____ 11. enough   The sink is full enough.

____ 12. heavy   We moved all the heavy boxes.

REVIEW WORDS

____ *13. town   ____ 17. about   ____ *21. meant

____ *14. hour   ____ 18. sound   ____ *22. bread

____ *15. now   ____ 19. brown   ____ 23. weather

____ *16. house   ____ 20. south   ____ 24. sense

Challenge Words

____ 25. method   What is the best method to solve the problem?

____ 26. probably   It will probably be sunny tomorrow.

____ 27. business   The family owned a clock repair business.

____ 28. energy   The sun and the wind are sources of energy.

Name: _____

enough

nothing

rough

heavy

1. _____

2. _____

3. _____

4. _____

5. _____

6. _____

7. _____

8. _____

1. _____

2. _____

3. _____

4. _____

5. _____

6. _____

7. _____

weather
don't
bread

8. _____

9. _____

10. _____

Name: _____

1. _____

2. _____

3. _____

4. _____

5. _____

6. _____

7. _____

8. _____

9. _____

10. _____

nothing

heavy

nowhere

1. _____

2. _____

3. _____

4. _____

5. _____

6. _____

7. _____

8. _____

9. _____

10. _____

rough

enough

A.M.

Name: _____

Write words with the ending **ing** by doubling the last consonant of the base word.

stepping _____

_____

_____

_____

_____

_____

Write words with the ending **ing** by dropping the final **e** of the base word.

driving _____

_____

_____

_____

_____

_____

Write words with the ending **ing** by just adding **ing**.

chewing _____

_____

_____

_____

_____

_____

NEW WORDS

____ *1. oil   Many machines need oil often.

____ *2. enjoy   They will enjoy the new book.

____ *3. square   He drew a circle inside a square.

____ *4. real   Real gems were on display in the museum.

____ 5. leave   Please leave your shoes at the door.

____ 6. voice   Her voice was too loud for the classroom.

____ 7. ground   She found an interesting rock on the ground.

____ 8. deep   The children fell into a deep sleep.

____ *9. woman   I saw one man and one woman.

____ *10. women   I saw two men and two women.

____ 11. above   Look on the shelf above the books.

____ 12. busy   He was busy doing his homework.

REVIEW WORDS

____ *13. boys'   ____ 17. please   ____ *21. rough

____ *14. men's   ____ 18. girl's   ____ *22. nothing

____ *15. boy's   ____ 19. seem   ____ 23. heavy

____ *16. puppy's   ____ 20. puppies'   ____ 24. enough

Challenge Words

____ 25. general   You expressed the general idea. Now add details.

____ 26. alone   He was alone in the room.

____ 27. figure   Each artist drew the figure of an animal.

____ 28. suppose   I suppose you already know the answer.

women

busy

above

woman

1. _____

2. _____

3. _____

4. _____

5. _____

6. _____

7. _____

8. _____

1. _____

2. _____

3. _____

4. _____

5. _____

6. _____

7. _____

haven't
nothing
enough

8. _____

9. _____

10. _____

Name: _____

1. _____

2. _____

3. _____

4. _____

5. _____

6. _____

7. _____

8. _____

9. _____

10. _____

heavy
above
woman

Name: _____

1. _____

2. _____

3. _____

4. _____

5. _____

6. _____

7. _____

busy
women
P.M.

8. _____

9. _____

10. _____

Name: _____

Write homophone pairs. You may want to use some of these words:
feat, knead, sea, right, weight, mane, hare, close, tale, new, weak, our

by _____   buy _____

two _____   too _____

_____   _____

_____   _____

_____   _____

_____   _____

_____   _____

_____   _____

NEW WORDS

____ *1. able   Horses are able to pull great weights.

____ *2. simple   Two plus two? That's simple!

____ *3. middle   He is the middle son in his family.

____ *4. title   The title made her want to read the book.

____ 5. uncle   Their uncle took them on the train.

____ 6. circle   A large circle was painted on the playground.

____ 7. July   The annual picnic was held in July.

____ 8. December   December 31 is the last day of the year.

____ *9. Wednesday   I went to a wedding on Wednesday.

____ *10. February   February is the shortest month.

____ 11. trouble   Use common sense to avoid trouble.

____ 12. touch   It felt strange to touch the lizard.

REVIEW WORDS

____ *13. enjoy   ____ 17. leave   ____ *21. women

____ *14. square   ____ 18. ground   ____ *22. woman

____ *15. real   ____ 19. voice   ____ 23. busy

____ *16. oil   ____ 20. deep   ____ 24. above

Challenge Words

____ 25. single   A single fish was in the tank.

____ 26. example   Please give an example.

____ 27. cattle   The cattle ate grasses on the range.

____ 28. capital   Austin is the capital of Texas.

Wednesday
touch
trouble
February

1. _____

2. _____

3. _____

4. _____

5. _____

6. _____

7. _____

8. _____

1. _____

2. _____

3. _____

4. _____

5. _____

6. _____

7. _____

won't
above
woman

8. _____

9. _____

10. _____

Name: _____

1. _____

2. _____

3. _____

4. _____

5. _____

6. _____

7. _____

8. _____

9. _____

10. _____

February
Wednesday
busy

1. _____

2. _____

3. _____

4. _____

5. _____

6. _____

7. _____

trouble
Wed.
touched

8. _____

9. _____

10. _____

Name:

Write words with the ending **ed** by doubling the last consonant of the base word.

tugged

_____

_____

_____

_____

_____

Write words with the ending **ed** by dropping the final **e** of the base word.

skated

_____

_____

_____

_____

_____

Write words with the ending **ed** by just adding **ed**.

melted

_____

_____

_____

_____

_____

NEW WORDS

____	*1. August	August is his favorite month.
____	*2. draw	They will draw illustrations for the chapter.
____	*3. fall	Don't fall off the wall.
____	*4. face	Feel the sun on your face.
____	5. pair	She wore a pair of bows in her hair.
____	6. April	The weather grew warm in April.
____	7. eleven	Four plus seven equals eleven.
____	8. author	The author spoke to a large audience.
____	*9. aunt	Her aunt and uncle live in Florida.
____	*10. post	We mailed the package at the post office.
____	11. almost	They have finished almost all their work.
____	12. January	They started the new calendar on January 1.

REVIEW WORDS

____ *13. title	____ 17. uncle	____ *21. February
____ *14. able	____ 18. December	____ *22. Wednesday
____ *15. simple	____ 19. July	____ 23. touch
____ *16. middle	____ 20. circle	____ 24. trouble

Challenge Words

____	25. opposite	Rough is the opposite of smooth.
____	26. produce	Midwestern states produce corn and wheat.
____	27. possible	Two answers seemed possible.
____	28. around	Put tape around the package.

Name: _____

post
almost
January
aunt

1. _____

2. _____

3. _____

4. _____

5. _____

6. _____

7. _____

8. _____

1. _____

2. _____

3. _____

4. _____

5. _____

6. _____

7. _____

8. _____

9. _____

10. _____

you'll
touch
Wednesday

Name: _____

1. _____

2. _____

3. _____

4. _____

5. _____

6. _____

7. _____

8. _____

9. _____

10. _____

February
aunt
postcard

1. _____

2. _____

3. _____

4. _____

5. _____

6. _____

7. _____

8. _____

9. _____

10. _____

January
almost
Aug.

Name:

_____

Write words that rhyme with **all**. They may end with **all**, **aul**, or **awl**. Underline each word that ends with **all**.

<u>squall</u>

Paul

Week 23

____ *1. flying
____ *2. fries
____ *3. puppies
____ *4. cried
____ 5. week
____ 6. hurrying
____ 7. speak
____ 8. speed
____ *9. often
____ *10. ready
____ 11. become
____ 12. listen

Week 27

____ *37. enjoy
____ *38. square
____ *39. real
____ *40. oil
____ 41. leave
____ 42. ground
____ 43. voice
____ 44. deep
____ *45. women
____ *46. woman
____ 47. busy
____ 48. above

Week 25

____ *13. town
____ *14. hour
____ *15. now
____ *16. house
____ 17. about
____ 18. sound
____ 19. brown
____ 20. south
____ *21. meant
____ *22. bread
____ 23. weather
____ 24. sense

Week 28

____ *49. title
____ *50. able
____ *51. simple
____ *52. middle
____ 53. uncle
____ 54. December
____ 55. July
____ 56. circle
____ *57. February
____ *58. Wednesday
____ 59. touch
____ 60. trouble

Week 26

____ *25. boys' (two boys' heads)
____ *26. men's
____ *27. boy's (one boy's nose)
____ *28. puppy's
        (one puppy's tail)
____ 29. please
____ 30. girl's (one girl's hat)
____ 31. seem
____ 32. puppies'
        (five puppies' mother)
____ *33. rough
____ *34. nothing
____ 35. heavy
____ 36. enough

Challenge Words

Week 23
rather, level, position, system

Week 25
mountains, flour, flower, thousand

Week 26
business, method, energy, probably

Week 27
figure, alone, general, suppose

Week 28
example, capital, single, cattle

Name: _____

1. _____

2. _____

3. _____

4. _____

5. _____

6. _____

7. _____

8. _____

9. _____

10. _____

11. _____

12. _____

Name:

_____

1. The women were hurrying to be reddy on time.

_____

2. The plane was flying high abuv the grownd at a very fast spede.

_____

3. The mother dog had four brown puppies. One puppy's ear was white.

_____

4. Her unkle offen speeks in a loud voice.

_____

5. The two boy's house is in the midle of toun.

Write these words in alphabetical order. In some words, you will need to look at the first, second, third, fourth, and fifth letters:

speak, above, women, leave, means, brown, week, circle, woman, hour, puppies, house, uncle, speed, trouble, bread, February, busy, meant, Wednesday

1. _____

2. _____

3. _____

4. _____

5. _____

6. _____

7. _____

8. _____

9. _____

10. _____

11. _____

12. _____

13. _____

14. _____

15. _____

16. _____

17. _____

18. _____

19. _____

20. _____

Dictionary and Personal Word List

Name: _____

A

__ able
__ about
__ above
__ across
__ add
__ almost
__ along
__ also
__ any
__ April
__ August
__ aunt
__ author
_____
_____
_____
_____
_____

B

__ become
__ before
__ bird
__ board
__ boat
__ body
__ book
__ bought
__ box
__ boy's
__ boys'
__ bread
__ break
__ breath
__ bridge
__ brings
__ brown
__ burn
__ busy

C

__ cares
__ carry
__ cent
__ chance
__ change
__ chased
__ check
__ chief
__ choose
__ circle
__ city
__ climb
__ closing
__ clothes
__ cold
__ country
__ cried
__ cross
_____
_____
_____
_____

D

__ dead
__ December
__ deep
__ die
__ dishes
__ draw
__ due
__ during
_____
_____
_____
_____
_____
_____
_____
_____
_____
_____

Dictionary and Personal Word List

Name:
_____

E

— <u>early</u>
— eat
— edge
— eggs
— <u>eighteen</u>
— eleven
— empty
— <u>English</u>
— enjoy
— <u>enough</u>
_____
_____
_____
_____
_____
_____
_____
_____
_____
_____
_____

F

— face
— facts
— fall
— fancy
— <u>father</u>
— <u>February</u>
— feel
— feet
— felt
— <u>few</u>
— <u>field</u>
— fifteen
— fifty
— fine
— fire
— first
— flat
— <u>floor</u>
— flying
— foot
— <u>fold</u>
— forty
— <u>fourteen</u>
— <u>fourth</u>

— fresh
— Friday
— fries
— <u>fruit</u>
— fry
— <u>full</u>
— funny
_____
_____
_____
_____
_____
_____
_____
_____
_____
_____

G

— gave
— girl's
— glad
— glasses
— <u>gold</u>
— grass
— ground
— <u>group</u>
— grow
— grew
— <u>guard</u>
— <u>guess</u>
— <u>guide</u>
_____
_____
_____
_____
_____
_____

Name: _____

H

— hair
— half
— hands
— happy
— head
— health
— heated
— heavy
— held
— hold
— horse
— hour
— house
— hurrying
— _____
— _____
— _____
— _____
— _____
— _____
— _____
— _____

I, J, K

— inside
— instead
— January
— judge
— July
— June
— kept
— key
— kings
— knew
— _____
— _____
— _____
— _____
— _____
— _____
— _____
— _____

L

— land
— large
— laugh
— learn
— leave
— led
— length
— light
— listen
— live
— living
— loose
— lose
— lost
— low
— _____
— _____
— _____
— _____
— _____

M

— main
— many
— March
— marked
— match
— May
— mean
— meant
— men's
— middle
— milk
— mind
— missing
— Monday
— money
— month
— moon
— mother
— must
— _____
— _____
— _____
— _____

Dictionary and Personal Word List

Name: _____

N, O	P	Q, R	S
— near	— page	— quickly	— sand
— need	— pair	— quite	— Saturday
— night	— passes	— racing	— school
— nine	— pencil	— raised	— scratch
— none	— phone	— read	— sea
— north	— planned	— ready	— search
— note	— plants	— real	— seem
— nothing	— please	— rich	— send
— November	— plenty	— rocks	— sense
— now	— post	— rough	— sent
— October	— pretty	_____	— September
— often	— prove	_____	— shapes
— oil	— pull	_____	— shared
— other	— puppies	_____	— shoes
— over	— puppies'	_____	— should
_____	— puppy's	_____	— sight
_____	— push	_____	— sign
_____	_____	_____	— simple
_____	_____	_____	— since
_____	_____	_____	— sitting
_____	_____	_____	— sixty
_____	_____	_____	— sky
_____	_____	_____	— snow
_____	_____	_____	— soft

__ <u>sold</u>

__ song

__ soon

__ sound

__ south

__ speak

__ speed

__ spent

__ square

__ stands

__ starring

__ states

__ stayed

__ sticks

__ still

__ stood

__ store

__ <u>straight</u>

__ strange

__ street

__ strong

__ <u>suit</u>

__ Sunday

T

__ tail

__ team

__ thick

__ thin

__ third

__ thirteen

__ those

__ three

__ throat

__ Thursday

__ <u>tie</u>

__ title

__ <u>toe</u>

__ <u>touch</u>

__ <u>toward</u>

__ town

__ trip

__ <u>trouble</u>

__ <u>truth</u>

__ <u>Tuesday</u>

Dictionary and Personal Word List

Name:

U, V

__ uncle
__ under
__ used
__ voice
_____
_____
_____
_____
_____
_____
_____
_____
_____
_____
_____
_____
_____
_____

W

__ wait
__ wear
__ weather
__ Wednesday
__ week
__ which
__ white
__ whose
__ wind
__ with
__ woman
__ women
__ won't
__ woods
__ would
__ worse
__ worst
__ worth
__ writing
__ wrong
_____
_____
_____
_____

X, Y, Z